SAFETY FIRST

Safety at Home

Joanne Mattern
ABDO Publishing Company

visit us at
www.abdopub.com

Published by Abdo Publishing Company 4940 Viking Drive, Edina, Minnesota 55435.
Copyright © 1999 by Abdo Consulting Group, Inc. International copyrights reserved in all
countries. No part of this book may be reproduced in any form without written permission
from the publisher.

Printed in the United States.

Photo credits: Peter Arnold, Inc., SuperStock

Edited by Julie Berg
Contributing editor Morgan Hughes
Graphics by Linda O'Leary

Library of Congress Cataloging-in-Publication Data

Mattern, Joanne, 1963-
    Safety at home / Joanne Mattern.
    p. cm. -- (Safety first)
    Includes index.
    Summary: Examines potential dangers in the home, including knives and other
kitchen tools, electric appliances, and guns, and discusses ways to behave safely.
    ISBN 1-57765-071-9
    1. Home accidents--Prevention--Juvenile literature. 2. Children's accidents--
Prevention--Juvenile literature. 3. Safety education--Juvenile literature.
[1. Safety.] I. Title. II. Series.
  HV675.5.M37 1999
  613.6--dc21

98-5530
CIP
AC

Contents

Safety First!

It's likely that you spend a good part of your day at home. That's why it's important to know how to stay safe there.

Staying safe means you won't get hurt. You won't get in trouble. And you will keep other people from getting hurt or in trouble, too!

How can you stay safe at home? The best way is to follow the rules and think before you act. This book will show you how to put safety first while you are at home.

Opposite page: Have fun, but remember to put safety first.

Stoves and Ovens

Your kitchen stove gets very hot. Never touch the burners on top of the stove, even if they are turned off. If there are pots on the stove, be sure their handles are turned toward the back. It's easy to knock over a hot pot if its handle is sticking out.

If you are wearing a shirt with long sleeves, push the sleeves up so they won't touch the burners and catch fire. If you have long hair, tie it back before you use the stove.

Turn pot handles toward the back to avoid accidents.

Ovens are hot, too. Always use a **pot holder** to put food in the oven or to take it out. Don't touch the oven racks or the pan with your bare hands.

If you use a **microwave oven**, let the food cool for a few minutes before you remove it. Take the cover off the dish carefully, so the hot steam rises away from your face.

Use a wooden spoon when you're stirring something hot.

Using Kitchen Tools

Stoves and ovens aren't the only **dangerous** things in the kitchen. You need to be careful when you use knives and other tools, too.

It's best to let an adult use a knife. If you have to cut something, be sure to cut *away* from your body. Keep your fingertips away from the knife. And always **concentrate** on what you are doing. Don't fool around when you have a knife in your hand!

Kitchen tools such as can openers and mixers have sharp parts that can cut you. Ask an adult to show you how to use them. Make sure you follow all the rules!

Opposite page: Watch out for your fingers when cutting with a knife.

Even the toaster can be **dangerous**! Never stick a knife or other sharp objects into a toaster to take out a piece of bread. Unplug the toaster and use your fingers once it has cooled. Or ask an adult to help.

Water and Electricity Don't Mix

Your kitchen might have lots of **appliances** on the counter. It's important to keep them away from the sink. Many kitchen devices are **electric**. If one falls in the sink or gets wet, you can get a very bad **shock**.

Always use kitchen appliances away from water. If you have to wash an electric machine, unplug it and wipe it with a wet dish rag. Be careful not to touch the wires with your wet hands!

Never use appliances near a sink.

Electric machines can also be found in the bathroom. Be careful when you use a hair dryer or other tools that are powered by electricity. Never use one while you are sitting in the bathtub or using the shower.

Be careful when helping in the kitchen.

In the Bathroom

Do you know what one of the most **dangerous** places in the bathroom is? The **medicine cabinet**!

The medicine cabinet has lots of pills and other kinds of medicine. Some of these medicines will help you if you are not feeling well. But some of them can make you very sick. Even good medicines can be bad if you take too much of them.

Some pills come in bright colors. They look like candy. But they're not! Never eat or drink any medicine because it looks good or tastes good. You should only take medicine that an adult gives you.

Medicine cabinets also contain razor blades. These are very sharp and can give you a bad cut. Don't touch razor blades.

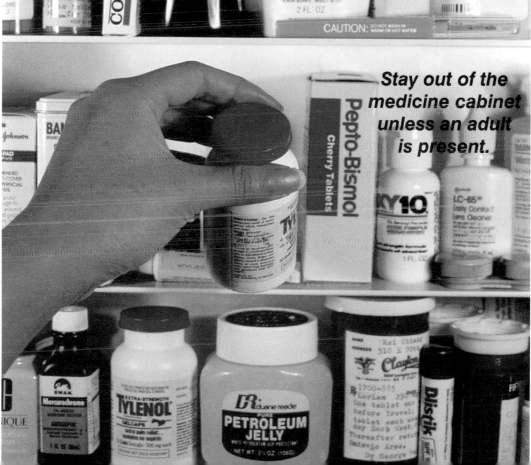

Stay out of the medicine cabinet unless an adult is present.

Danger under the Sink

There might be lots of interesting bottles, cans, and boxes under the sinks in your bathroom and kitchen. But you should never touch any of them. Many of these products are **poisonous**. Eating or drinking them can make you very sick. Some of them can burn your skin if you touch them.

Some people keep **insecticides**, **pesticides**, or **gasoline** in their garage, basement, or shed. All of these things can make you sick. You should never touch them!

Opposite page:
WARNING:
Never play with things
from under a sink.

Fire Safety

There are many ways to keep your home safe from fire. You can help by never playing with matches. Matches are not toys!

You should also ask your parents to keep a **fire extinguisher** in the kitchen. Sometimes a fire can start while you are cooking. Having a fire extinguisher will help you put the fire out fast!

It is important to have **smoke detectors** and **carbon monoxide detectors**. You should have at least one on each floor and one near each bedroom. These detectors need batteries to work. Pick a special day, like your birthday or a holiday, to put in new batteries and test each detector.

smoke alarm   *fire extinguisher*

Practice escape routes with your family in case there is a fire. Talk to your parents about how to escape from every room. Choose a meeting place outside. And never go back into the house for anything, even to rescue a pet. Get out of the house as fast as you can!

Plan an escape route with your family.

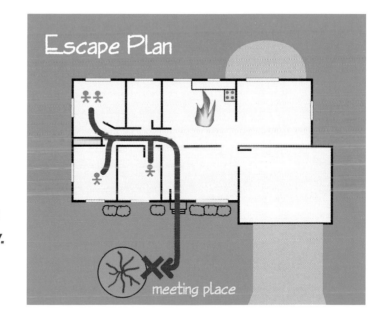

Escape Plan

meeting place

Gun Safety

Some people keep a gun in the house. Guns are very **dangerous** if they are not used safely. Never play with a gun. If the gun is loaded with bullets, it can go off. Someone could be hurt, or even killed. You can't tell if a gun is loaded by just looking at it. The best thing to do is leave the gun alone.

If your friends want to play with a gun, don't join them. You shouldn't even stay in the area in case the gun goes off by **accident**. Many children have been hurt or killed playing with guns. A gun is not a toy. Guns should always be locked away in a cabinet or gun case.

Opposite page:
Guns should always
be locked in a case.

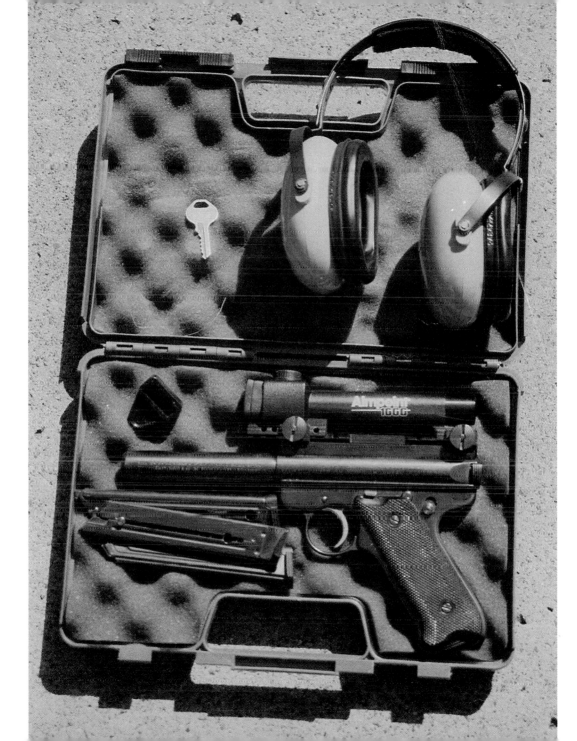

When You're Home Alone

Never tell a stranger that you are home alone. If someone you don't know comes to the door, pretend you aren't home. If a stranger calls and asks to talk to your parents, say, "They are busy now. Please leave your number and they will call you back."

A stranger might call and ask what your name is, or where you live or go to school. Don't answer these questions. Ask for the person's number and say your parents will call back. If you feel scared, it's okay to hang up.

Use the same caution when you are on the internet. Don't give out your home address. If you are in a chat room and don't like what people are saying, leave.

And always let your parents know what chat rooms you've been in and what sites you are visiting.

Never tell a stranger that you are home alone.

Glossary

Accident (AK-see-duhnt) - something that takes place without planning it.

Appliance (uh-PLY-unss) - a machine that does a particular job.

Carbon monoxide detector - a device that detects the odorless gas called carbon monoxide and warns people with an alarm.

Concentrate (KON-suhn-trate) - to pay attention.

Dangerous (DAYN-jur-us) - likely to cause harm; not safe.

Electric (ih-lek-TRICK) - a form of energy.

Fire extinguisher (FIRE ek-STING-gwish-ur) - a metal container with chemicals and water inside to put out a fire.

Gasoline (gass-uh-LEEN) - a liquid fuel used in cars and other machines to power them.

Insecticide (in-SEK-tuh-side) - a chemical used to kill insects.

Medicine cabinet (MED-uh-suhn KAB-in-it) - a set of shelves that holds drugs used to treat illness.

Microwave oven (MY-kroh-wave UHV-uhn) - an oven that cooks food quickly from the inside out.

Pesticide (PESS-tuh-side) - a chemical used to kill insects and other pests.

Poisonous (POI-zuhn-uss) - something that can harm someone if it is swallowed, breathed, or touched.

Pot holder - a piece of cloth used to hold hot pots or other hot kitchen items.

Shock (SHOK) - the violent effect of an electric current passing through someone's body.

Smoke detector (SMOHK di-TEK-tur) - a device that warns people of smoke or fire by letting out a loud sound.

Internet Sites

Bicycling Safety
http://www.cam.org/~skippy/sites/cycling/SafetyLinks.html
Stories, studies, statistics, and tips on everything from safe cycling practices to maintenance. Special interest sections for kids and parents, and links to many interesting sites!

Safety Tips for Kids on the Internet
http://www.fbi.gov/kids/internet/internet.htm
The FBI has set up a "safety tips for the internet" website. It has very good information about how to protect yourself online.

National School Safety Center
http://www.nssc1.org/
This site provides training and resources for preventing school crime and violence.

Home Safety
http://www.safewithin.com/homesafe/
This site helps to make the home more secure, info on the health of the home environment and other safety resources.
These sites are subject to change.

Pass It On

Educate readers around the country by passing on information you've learned about staying safe. Share your little-known facts and interesting stories. Tell others about bike riding, school experiences, and any other stuff you'd like to discuss. We want to hear from you!
To get posted on the ABDO Publishing Company website E-mail us at
"adventure@abdopub.com"
Download a free screen saver at www.abdopub.com

Index